NATURE

The Tuatara

Brian O'Flaherty
Photographs by Rod Morris

Cover photograph: Gem nudibranch by Iain A. Anderson.
Back cover photographs: (l–r) ice plant, cat's eye snails by Brian O'Flaherty.
Contents page photograph by Iain A. Anderson.

Other titles in the Nature Kids series:
Seals and sea lions
The Albatross
The Kea
The Kiwi
The Penguin
The Tuatara
The Weta

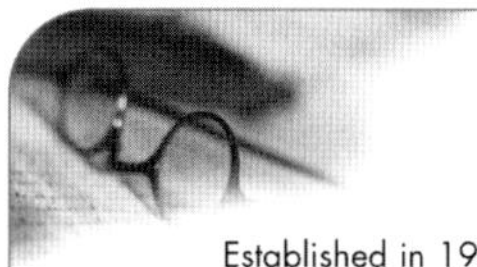

Published by Reed Children's Books, an imprint of Reed Publishing (NZ) Ltd, 39 Rawene Rd, Birkenhead, Auckland 10.
Associated companies, branches and representatives throughout the world.

ISBN 1 86948 725 7
First published 2003

Edited by Carolyn Lagahetau
Designed by Helen Barker

Printed in New Zealand

Contents

Who, what, where?

Tuatara are reptiles.
Reptiles are animals with cold blood and scaly skin.
They lay eggs.

Tuatara live only in New Zealand.
Years ago, they lived all over the country.
Now there are not many left.

Tuatara is a Maori name.
It means 'spiny back' or
'peaks on the back'.

Family tree

Tuatara belong to the same class as tortoises, turtles, snakes, lizards and crocodiles.
They are in a group called 'beak-headed reptiles'.
There are two species of tuatara: northern tuatara and Brother's tuatara.
Northern tuatara is the most common tuatara.

Northern tuatara have a brownish skin.

The tuatara has been on Earth since dinosaur times.

There are only about 400 Brother's tuatara left. They live on an island in Cook Strait.

Good looks

Tuatara can bite hard.

Tuatara become adults at about 13 years old. They can live to over 60 years old.

According to Maori legend, tuatara and lizards are children of Punga, the god of all things ugly.

Adults can grow up to 60 centimetres long and weigh about 500 grams.

Scaly skin
Spiny back and tail
Big mouth and strong jaws
Strong claws

Extra eye

The tuatara has a third eye, on top of the brain.
You can see the eye on baby tuatara, but as they grow it gets covered with scales.
The eye isn't used for seeing.

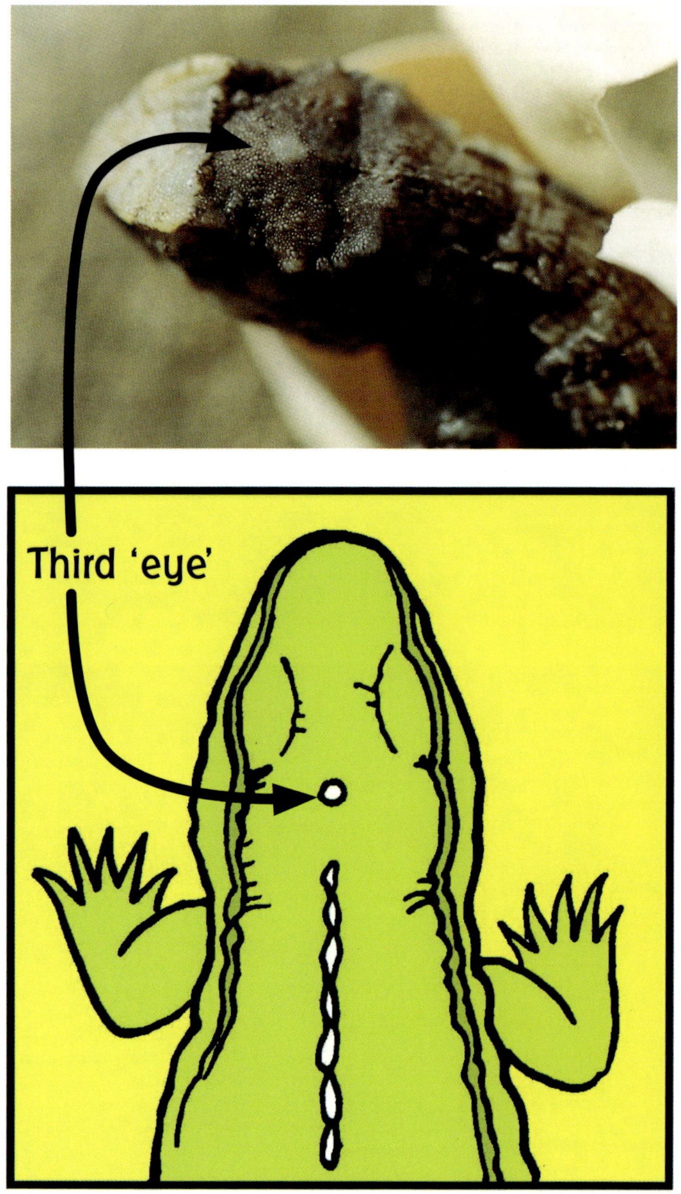

No one is sure what the eye is for. It can sense light, and may help tuatara find their way home.

Cool dudes

Reptiles have cold blood, so they need warm temperatures to be active. Tuatara spend the coldest months in a kind of deep sleep.
When it is cold, adult tuatara can slow their body down.
When it is warmer, the body speeds up, and the heart rate and breathing get quicker.

A tuatara's heart rate can drop to just one beat a minute. They will take a breath only every few minutes.

Sounds and signals

Tuatara can make croaking noises.
They usually croak when fighting other tuatara.
Tuatara mostly use 'body talk' — moving and nodding.

The tuatara nods her head to say she's female.

To attract females, the male makes himself look as big as possible. He lifts himself up on his legs, with his spines standing up straight.

Male tuatara.

Home, sweet home

Tuatara are most active at night. They sleep in burrows during the day. Some burrows they dig themselves.

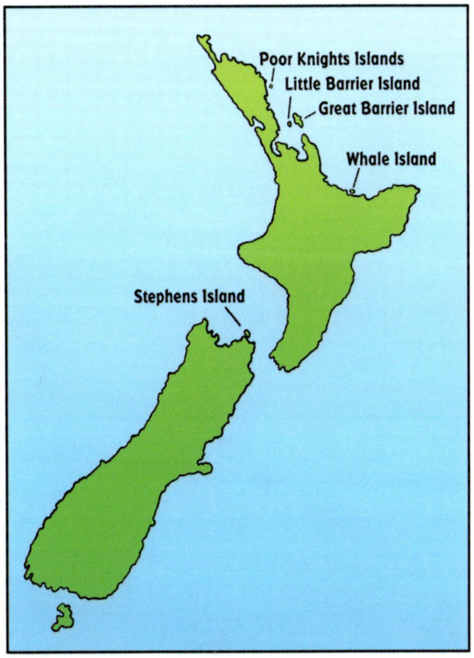

Sometimes tuatara share burrows made by nesting seabirds.

Tuatara live on islands around New Zealand. Once tuatara lived all over New Zealand. Today they live only on about 30 offshore islands in Northland, the Bay of Plenty and Cook Strait.

Dinnertime!

Tuatara have plenty of sharp teeth. They hunt and eat food at night. But they like to sit in the sun during the day, as the warmth helps digest this food. If there is danger, they will return to their burrows.

Tuatara are carnivores (meat eaters).

R. Morris

Tuatara eat:

- Earthworms
- Insects (weta, moths, beetles)
- Lizards
- Seabird eggs and chicks
- Snails
- Spiders
- Slaters

Adult tuatara sometimes eat seabird eggs.

Eggs

Tuatara eggs have leathery shells.

Tuatara start to mate when they are about 20 years old.
The female usually lays her eggs in October or November.
She will lay 8 to 13 eggs in a tunnel. Then she leaves them.

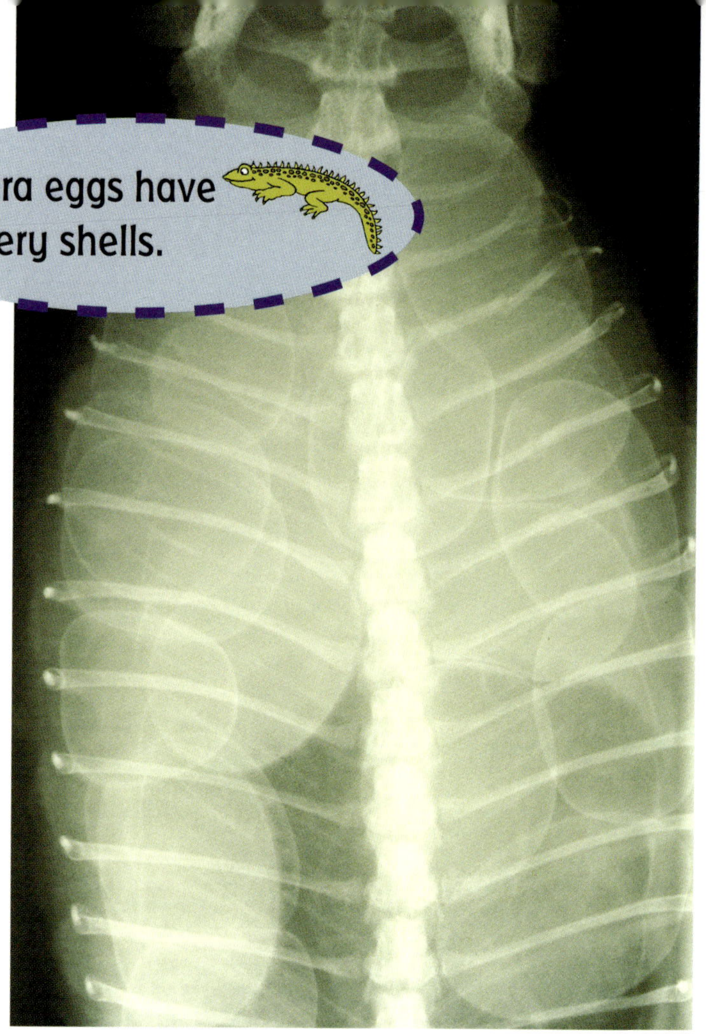

This X-ray shows eggs inside a female tuatara.

The female tuatara finds a quiet place and digs a small tunnel. Then she lays her eggs.

Hatchlings

It is at least a year before tuatara hatch from their eggs.
The baby tuatara breaks the egg and leaves the burrow.
On the surface, hatchlings shelter under rocks and logs.

Sometimes hatchlings hide up trees.

Hatchlings can move quickly.

Danger!

Long ago, the only creatures that ate tuatara were birds, like black-backed gulls, kingfishers or moreporks.
But when humans came to New Zealand, they brought new enemies for tuatara.
Rats, cats and wild pigs can easily catch the slow-moving tuatara.

Help save us

There used to be millions of tuatara, but there are not so many now. They are still in danger. Scientists keep some tuatara in zoos or other places to help them breed.

When hatchlings are old enough, they are returned to islands where there are no enemies.

The number of tuatara in these places is growing again.

Zoos are good places to see tuatara.

Some tuatara are kept in the Tuatarium at Southland Museum.

There are about 100,000 tuatara.

Index